Bullyi
and ASD:
The Perfect
Storm

Autism Partnership

Bullying and ASD: The Perfect Storm

Copyright © 2013 Autism Partnership

Published by: DRL Books Inc.
                   37 East 18th Street, 10th Floor
                   New York, NY 10003
                   Phone: 212-604-9637
                   Fax: 212-206-9329

Book Layout: PreMediaGlobal

Library of Congress Control Number: 2012935751
ISBN-13: 978-0-9836226-7-3
ISBN-10: 0-9836226-7-1

Table of Contents

Dealing with a Bully

Bullying has become a prominent issue in today's world. A recent survey of 400 parents conducted by Massachusetts Advocates for Children found that 88 percent of children with autism have been bullied at school.[1] Whether in the form of cyber bullying, verbal abuse or physical assault, we frequently hear terrible stories of students being tormented by peers. Bullying is not limited to just children and causes emotional and physical harm to people of all ages. In our experience counseling children and young adults with autism spectrum disorder (ASD), we have found that many express extreme worry and anxiety as a result of being bullied in social situations. Unable to change the situation and feeling vulnerable, they often communicate anger and sometimes fantasies of revenge by expressing a desire to have others feel the pain they have been experiencing. On rare occasions they act out toward others, either due to misunderstandings or lack of skills for dealing with complex social situations and express feeling justified in their conduct.

Bullying is not the same as teasing. Unlike friendly teasing, bullying is long-term torment that does not occur between social equals. Research on bullying suggests that while many factors can put someone at risk of being a target, bullies tend to choose victims they know their classmates will not defend.[2] Commonly, it affects those that are most vulnerable. All too often, children with ASD fall

[1] *www.disabilityscoop.com/2009/11/13/bullying*

[2] *www.hu ngtonpost.com/2012/03/28*

into this category. Perhaps because they are different in terms of behaviors, interests or even appearance, they have become prime targets for bullying. According to Julia Landau, senior autism center director at Massachusetts Advocates for Children, "Children with ASD are especially vulnerable targets because of the nature of their disability. Children on the spectrum are often viewed as atypical or different by their peers, and are generally unable to understand bullying incidents and protect themselves like other students due to the nature of ASD, which impacts communication, social and behavioral skills."[3] Children with ASD may even view the bully as a "friend" because they are unable to accurately read the social climate and are interested in receiving the attention. Children with ASD have trouble interpreting the motives of others and can be overly concrete in their understanding of language and behaviors. They can have difficulty making a distinction between something that occurred by accident or on purpose and may over or under react to a given situation.

There are numerous reasons that underlie bullying—to intimidate, receive attention, gain control or increase social status are just a few. Recent research has revealed that most bullies tend to have average or above-average levels of self-esteem, often have good leadership skills and have at least a small group of friends that support their behavior. Unsurprisingly, it was found that individuals who exhibit bullying behaviors tend to come from families that are less affectionate and communicative, utilize a punitive and rigid discipline style and receive little monitoring throughout the day. Individuals exhibiting bullying behavior may lack the skills to manage their emotions appropriately. Of course, positive reinforcement plays a role in the maintenance of bullying behavior as the bully

[3]*www.disabilityscoop.com/2009/11/13/bullying*

may be rewarded for his/her conduct through tangible (i.e., stolen designer sneakers) and intangible outcomes (i.e., increased notoriety). Of course, identifying factors that contribute to someone becoming a bully does not excuse the conduct. As adults we must send a clear message to our youth that no one should have to suffer at the hands of a bully!

Traditional Strategies

Focusing on the Bully

A number of strategies have been employed to decrease bullying. A common approach is for parents or school personnel to confront, lecture and punish the bully. Often there are threats of stronger action if the bullying persists. Another approach is sensitivity training aimed at helping the bully understand why children with ASD behave the way they do. The rationale for sensitivity training is to increase acceptance of other peoples' differences.

How effective are these approaches? In some cases, focusing on the bully may actually work. However, sensitivity and acceptance does not often develop from a course or lecture, and lack of understanding about why children with ASD act differently is not the only problem. Even worse, such traditional measures can make the bully resentful and secretive. The bully's behavior may morph into a different form that is every bit as destructive and dangerous. An alternative strategy is to focus on the victim rather than the bully.

Focusing on the Victim

A common approach is to encourage the victim to tell a teacher, principal or any adult who can provide protection from the bully. Clearly, making a report is essential if the victim's safety is at risk. However, making a report may result in the bully escalating the persecution and going "underground."

Assertiveness training is often used to teach a victim to stand up to the bully. In a role play situation, the victim practices telling the bully, "Stop" or "I don't like that." The target of bullying may be taught to inform the bully, "You're not being a good friend and the way you're treating me is wrong!" It is not difficult to predict the effectiveness of this strategy. It often results in the bully intensifying his or her behavior, resulting in further harm to the victim.

Some recommend befriending the bully, to disarm them by treating an enemy as a friend. Even if this could be effective with the general population, individuals with ASD often have compromised social skills and typically do not know how to be a friend to a willing peer, let alone a resistant or challenging individual.

Another approach is to teach the victim to simply ignore the bully. The victim is taught to understand that bullies torment for a reason, often hoping for a reaction. The rationale is that ignoring and not reacting will cause the bully to stop. While this may work in some cases, it should be suggested with EXTREME caution. An obvious problem with ignoring is that the bully may escalate his behavior until it is impossible for the victim to ignore. In such situations, the bully will be reinforced for increased levels of provocative and aggressive behavior.

A second potential problem with ignoring is that although the victim may ignore the bully, it is likely others will not. Peers often provide reinforcement to the bully through supportive attention or encouragement. Peers who want to make sure that they are not bullied may align with the bully. Thus, ignoring would not be an effective strategy since attention from the victim is somewhat irrelevant and not the only component serving to maintain the behavior.

Finally, most people simply are not good at ignoring undesirable behavior. Although they may try to act as if they are not paying attention, body language and facial expressions typically give them away. A victim's active, deliberate and obvious attempts not to pay attention can actually serve as a sufficient reaction for the bully. Even if the victim truly is able to functionally ignore the bully, the emotional impact is still palpable—feelings of humiliation, sadness and desperation. In the final analysis, ignoring should only be recommended with great caution.

Alternative Approaches

Let us say from the outset, there is absolutely no excuse for bullying. It is morally unacceptable and should not be allowed or tolerated. Regardless of a person's history and psychological background, there is no justification for bullying. Since traditional strategies are largely ineffective for children with ASD, let's think outside the box and consider other options.

Bullying vs. Teasing

It is important to determine whether the victim is really a target of bullying or may be misinterpreting the actions of others. Children often tease peers as part of typical social behavior. Just because someone says mean things doesn't necessarily mean he or she is a bully. Boys in particular can be brutal with comments such as: "you're stupid," "you're ugly," or "you suck." Such bantering is not intended to intimidate or control, it is simply jostling for social position among relative equals.

We may need to teach our children with ASD to understand this distinction. Similar actions can have very different meaning, depending on intention which requires interpreting context and subtle aspects of behavior. Highlighting and demonstrating the extremes (e.g., fist fights vs. high fives) may be a starting point. Progressing to more subtle discriminations (including not only what is said or done but who is saying it and under what circumstances) will help children with ASD understand the distinction between bullying and teasing, and interpreting the motives of others. It is certainly a difficult discrimination, but one that may need to be systematically taught.

Avoiding the Bully

Developing a strategy of avoidance is another option. Making attempts to stay away from the bully during breaks, lunch or in class may be helpful. Helping the victim identify where the bully hangs out and to avoid those situations can often reduce unpleasant encounters.

Understanding Bullying

It may be helpful for children with ASD to understand a bully's behavior. Naturally, this would be based on the victim's level of comprehension. Helping a victim understand that bullies are seeking a reaction because of their desire to control the behaviors of others may provide motivation to the victim to change his or her typical response.

Alternatively, helping a child with ASD understand which behaviors (e.g., perseveration, stereotypic behavior, lecturing) create ammunition for or trigger a bully, and teaching him or her to refrain, in certain situations, from engaging in these behaviors may be helpful.

Stress Management

We have found that teaching children coping and relaxation strategies can be effective. Anxiety and stress can make a bad situation even worse. Learning to mentally go to a calm and peaceful place (e.g., imagining watching a favorite movie, listening to a cheerful song, eating a favorite food, etc.) can put children with ASD in a more relaxed mood and help them cope with the stress they experience in the presence of the bully. This may help them to not overreact, decrease the likelihood of engaging in behaviors that "trigger" the bully, and to feel less hurt by the bully's behavior.

Peer Tutor

One of the most successful strategies is to enlist a peer tutor. For boys it is often the highly successful and intelligent athlete. Such a tutor must be EXTREMELY cool, well respected and socially influential. An incentive that has worked well for motivating youth to volunteer their time is the opportunity to earn community service hours. These peers are beneficial in two ways. First, they can be extremely valuable in helping teach much-needed social skills in a truly authentic way. Since they are ultra-cool and tuned into adolescent ways and pop culture, they know what to teach (actions, language, mannerisms, music, movies, clothes, etc.). Perhaps more importantly, they offer protection! Other students simply won't mess with them or the student they are mentoring.

Other Considerations

Taking a Look Inward

When evaluating situations involving children with ASD being bullied, it is important to look at our own behavior as adults to determine if we are inadvertently contributing to the problem. It may be necessary to change our behavior to help defuse situations in which a child is being victimized by a bully. This in no way is meant to condone bullying. However, the reality is that sometimes adult behavior may facilitate bullying. So it is important to identify and change environmental antecedents (our behavior) that may contribute to bullying.

Adult behavior can create resentment within the peers of a child with ASD. It can be aggravating to peers when we make unnecessary accommodations, enforce different rules, allow interruptions to teaching, or avoid addressing behavior problems. Other students might ask: "Why doesn't he have to sit in his seat?", "Why doesn't he have to follow the same rules?", "Why don't you get mad at him?" Every effort should be made to treat students with ASD similar to other students. Making overabundant accommodations for them often is not helpful and can be extremely aggravating to peers, inadvertently promoting bullying responses.

Breaking down Barriers

Attempting to reduce the distinction between children with ASD and their peers is also worth considering. For example, a barrier between children with ASD and the larger peer community is created when those children have widely different interests, dress differently, or behave in an odd, aggressive or annoying manner.

Facilitating children with ASD to be less identifiably "uncool" may be extremely helpful. Appearance, behavior and interests can go a long way! Such a strategy may not prevent bullying, but it may diminish the child being socially ostracized and open them more readily to the socially supportive (and protective) forces of the larger peer group and ultimately create greater opportunity for genuine social reciprocity.

Students with ASD engage in behaviors that may be provocative to peers and especially to bullies. Being aggressive and rude, screaming when they lose, or laughing for no reason can be extremely annoying. These behaviors need to be addressed not only because they directly interfere with learning but because they can be offensive to peers.

Social awkwardness can also be problematic. Perseveration on an unusual or narrow range of topics (e.g., insects, trains, dinosaurs, etc.), invasion of personal space, and grabbing peers' possessions can be annoying. Addressing these behaviors programmatically is essential to pave the way for positive interactions with peers.

Perhaps the most important strategy is to help children with ASD learn to develop MEANINGFUL FRIENDSHIPS! When children have true friendships they are less vulnerable to bullying. The likelihood of being either drawn to or hurt by bullies is greatly reduced. By increasing their quality of life, we may also reduce the impact of bullying experiences. A social support and protective system is developed.

The development of meaningful social connections will require helping children improve their social skills. Learning to read social situations and responding to them accordingly is a vital skill. Becoming comfortable in conversation, staying on topic, maintaining conversational flow, and making appropriate conversational transitions creates social opportunity and increases social success.

Learning how to compromise and negotiate will increase children's abilities to navigate the social world. Obviously, these are critical but difficult skills to teach and to learn. It requires both skilled teachers and a functional and comprehensive social skills curriculum. It is the very reason why we wrote the book: *Crafting Connections: Contemporary Applied Behavior Analysis for Enriching the Social Lives of Persons with Autism Spectrum Disorder.* We highly recommend that parents and teachers utilize a guide book such as this to provide teaching strategies and curriculum that may help children with Autism Spectrum Disorder develop the social skills necessary to reduce their vulnerability and improve resiliency.